The Power of Water

Written by Paki Carter

Earth is always changing.

Water can change the land.

Let's look at some changes made by water.

Water from storms makes changes.
The rain storm lasts a long time.
The river gets higher.

The water changes the land.

Water in rivers makes changes.
A river flows through a canyon.
The canyon gets deeper.

The river changes the land.

Water in oceans makes changes.
Ocean waves keep hitting
the cliffs.
The cliffs wear away.

The waves change the land.

Water as ice makes changes.
The ice builds up.
It moves across the land.

The ice changes the land.

Earth is always changing.

Water can change the land.
Have you seen any of these
changes?